POVERTY
Responding Like Jesus

POVERTY
Responding Like Jesus

EDITED BY

Kenneth R. Himes, OFM, and Conor M. Kelly

IN COOPERATION WITH

The Church in the 21st Century Center

BOSTON COLLEGE

PARACLETE PRESS
BREWSTER, MASSACHUSETTS

2018 First printing

Poverty: Responding Like Jesus

Copyright © 2018 by The Church in the 21st Century Center

ISBN 978-1-61261-682-7

The excerpts quoted in chapters 2, 3, 4, 5, 6, 8, 9, 10, 11, 12, 13, and 14 are copyrighted by their respective publishers and are used with permission.

The Paraclete Press name and logo (dove on cross) are trademarks of Paraclete Press, Inc.

Library of Congress Cataloging-in-Publication Data

Names: Himes, Kenneth R., 1950- editor.
Title: Poverty : responding like Jesus / edited by Kenneth R. Himes, OFM, and
    Conor M. Kelly.
Description: Brewster, MA : Paraclete Press, Inc., 2018.
Identifiers: LCCN 2018004156 | ISBN 9781612616827 (trade paper)
Subjects: LCSH: Church work with the poor—Catholic Church. |
    Poverty—Religious aspects—Catholic Church.
Classification: LCC BX2347.8.P66 P68 2018 | DDC 261.8/325—dc23
LC record available at https://lccn.loc.gov/2018004156

10 9 8 7 6 5 4 3 2 1

Published by Paraclete Press
Brewster, Massachusetts
www.paracletepress.com

Printed in the United States of America

Contents

POVERTY
Responding Like Jesus

POVERTY AND CHRISTIAN DISCIPLESHIP

BY KENNETH R. HIMES, OFM

Poverty is a central issue both inside and outside the Church. From the moment of his election, Pope Francis has emphasized the vision of a "Church that is poor and for the poor." At the same time, growing economic inequality makes headlines across the globe. This book examines the role of the Church, and each faithful Christian, in relation to poverty. From the outset, the Christian community has wrestled with the realities of poverty and the poor. For that reason, a strong focus of this volume is placed on the biblical and theological roots of the Church's enduring commitment to care for the poor.

Jesus often preached parables that touched upon the reality of poverty in the experience of his listeners. In the Acts of the Apostles, there are scenes of the early Church struggling with how to think about possessions, poor widows in the community, and the proper attitude toward material wealth. In several letters Paul wrote about collecting money for the poor Jerusalem community, along with the scandal of communal meals at Corinth when rich and poor were divided from each other. And James scolded a community that overlooked its poor members while fawning over the rich.

Later Christians—hermits, theologians, monks, mendicants, mystics, social reformers, and spiritual writers—have added their voices to the discussion of poverty within the tradition. At times praised as a virtue and blessed as a condition, at other times opposed as a social evil and cursed as a burden, poverty has elicited many kinds of reactions among the followers of Christ. In the essays in this issue we present some of that diversity of viewpoint among believers.

THE FORMS OF POVERTY

In everyday conversation poverty usually means material poverty, the lack of goods that most of us need to experience a reasonable measure of security from hunger, cold, storms, illness. Countless human beings have walked across the face of this planet who lacked such basic goods. Deprived of resources for meeting basic bodily needs, too many people throughout history have died from hunger, thirst, exposure to the elements, and treatable illness. We have material needs, and the inability to satisfy them is a terrible evil inflicted upon those who are materially poor.

There is also spiritual poverty in our world. One may have adequate material well-being yet suffer from a profound sense of isolation or marginalization, cut off from community, friendship, intimacy, love. There are those unfortunates plagued by mental and emotional suffering for whom the challenge of rising from bed is a daily struggle with depression, anxiety, grief, or despair. In our information society there are people whose lack of education keeps them on the margins of society even if they manage to put food on their tables and roofs over their heads. There are those with illnesses that separate them from the everyday interactions of those who are unburdened by disease. And as John Chrysostom reminds us in his reflections on the parable of the rich man and Lazarus, there are the affluent and materially comfortable who are truly poor, abounding in wealth, but starving in virtue; propped up with false security, yet their life is in peril; living a life of easy comfort, but finding no meaning in luxury.

Poverty has many guises, and while the external face of material deprivation is often the easiest to recognize it is not the only way that poverty appears in the human situation. While Christians must never be indifferent to the material poverty of our brothers and sisters, it is also true that Christian believers ought to be among the first to discern the signs of spiritual poverty, in our own lives and in the lives of those we encounter. The works of mercy are both spiritual and material.

A KEY DIFFERENCE

An important distinction within the tradition is that of voluntary versus involuntary poverty. From the earliest generations of the Christian community there were people who voluntarily made themselves materially poor for the sake of a spiritual good, whether that good be giving assistance to others, acquiring virtue, engaging in repentance, deepening one's prayer, or imitating Christ. Throughout the history of Christianity there have been men and women who freely took vows of poverty or simply made decisions to forsake material wealth for the sake of their faith. When done in freedom, with a clear understanding of the consequences, and after a period of mature reflection, such a decision has been praised and admired by others as an act of genuine discipleship.

However, there is also involuntary poverty, the poverty that is not chosen but imposed, that is not an evangelical ideal but a countersign to the dignity of the human person. Involuntary poverty can corrupt our inner life even as it makes our external life difficult. Unmet physical needs can crush the spirit of a person. Because we are integrated creatures, both bodily and spiritual, it is not possible to divide ourselves neatly. When we have a severe toothache we also turn impatient, ill-tempered, self-absorbed, and difficult. When we are in love the sun seems to shine brighter, the coffee tastes better, and there is a bounce to our step. Our inner and outer lives cannot easily be cut off from each other; there is a profound reciprocity between them. Voluntary poverty can liberate people to attain a life of authentic Christianity. Involuntary poverty can oppress people so as to prevent a truly human life.

POVERTY AND INEQUALITY

Yet another distinction to bear in mind when thinking about poverty is the difference between relative and absolute poverty. The latter can be defined in ways that are connected with the experience of radical deprivation whereby essential needs are neglected. Absolute poverty can refer to the failure to satisfy minimal levels of caloric intake, or the inability to find shelter adequate to prevent frostbite. Absolute poverty means the lack of material goods that permit daily subsistence. It entails a state of destitution that deprives a person of essential food, potable water, sanitation, shelter, health, and education. It refers not only to income but also to access to goods.

Tattered or shrunken as it may be, the safety net in most economically developed countries is meant to raise all people above the level of absolute poverty. The World Bank put a dollar figure on absolute poverty in the poorest nations, setting the standard at $1.25 per person per day. Of course, conditions in richer nations require a different standard. The United States sets its poverty standard, according to recent figures, at $15.15 per adult per day.

Relative poverty is a more difficult issue to define. It is determined with reference to social context. It is most commonly explained as the percentage of a population that has less than a certain proportion of a society's median income—for example, the percentage of the population that has less than 50 percent of the median income. Such a group may be designated as living in relative poverty. In short, relative poverty is really a way of talking about economic inequality.

Relative poverty is not about survival but whether a person is able to participate effectively in the life of the society. This is not a new idea. Even Adam Smith in his classic book *The Wealth of Nations* discussed poverty not as the inability to obtain adequate resources to sustain life, but as the lack of what a nation's customs determine to be a decent standard of living for the least well off.

INTELLECTUAL POVERTY AND SOLIDARITY WITH THE POOR

Intellectual poverty is a true curse. It is to know the truth of the biblical proverb, "without a vision the people perish." To take away people's hope, to tell them that nothing is going to change, that nothing will get better, is to deny the gift of prophecy in the life of the Church. Prophets are about spreading hope, giving people a vision of where we are going, of what we are called to be. Intellectual poverty is the inability to even imagine a better society, to be incapable of aspiring to a future that is not simply a repetition of the past and present.

So much of life comes down to optics. If we do not see something, we do not respond to it. Unless the poor are real to us, we are not going to respond to them. And we live in a world where if we have a fair amount of resources it becomes pretty easy to live without a whole lot of direct contact with the poor. If we live in certain suburbs or neighborhoods we do not see the poor around us. If we go to private recreation areas and not public parks or pools we will not see the poor about us. We have created a society in which we can pretty much avoid the poor if we wish.

And so part of what solidarity with the poor entails is to see the world the way the poor see it. To face the world as it is for so many and not the safe haven we construct for ourselves is a gospel challenge. Solidarity entails coming to see things in a new way. We begin to see the world the poor see so that we can respond to obstacles the poor confront that we might otherwise not encounter. That becomes a vision that transforms our life. We realize there is another way to live, another set of priorities than the ones we have. We enter into the pain of the poor and we acquire a different vision of life, one that is closer to the perspective of the great men and women who have taken discipleship seriously.

The lessons of Catholic teaching have long included a special concern for the least well-off when assessing a community's commitment to justice. The test of a good community is not, "how well are those at the top doing?" The test is always, "how well are those at the bottom faring?" Can people find work that provides a living wage? Is there an adequate safety net for those who are too old or too young, who are chronically ill or temporarily incapacitated? As the Scripture attests, we are only as hospitable, generous, and decent a people as we are hospitable, generous, and decent to the poor among us. That's the standard of measurement, if we want to know what a good community is.

OPPOSITION OR DUAL OBLIGATION?

Finally, there is the issue of how today's Christians are to respond to the fact of the poor, both those close at hand and those halfway around the world. As many of the voices, like those of Dorothy Day or Peter Maurin, that can be heard in this book make clear, there is a profound obligation among Christians to provide for the poor through charity. Almsgiving has always been counted as being at the heart of the Christian life. Indeed, one of the most vivid of all portrayals of divine judgment is Matthew 25, where the sheep and goats are separated on the basis of whether or not Christ was recognized in the hungry, thirsty, naked, sick, or imprisoned brother and sister. Charity is at the center of Christian discipleship.

However, the argument has been made that charity can sometimes just be a bandage put on a problem that must be addressed at a deeper level. One description is that charity is equivalent to pulling drowning people out of a river. That's a necessary and life-giving service, to be sure. But justice goes upstream to find out why people are falling in the river in the first place and builds a safe bridge so that people can walk across the river. Therefore, charity becomes less necessary, less urgent.

Seen this way the advocates of justice can demean charity as simply saving victims while the work of justice is understood as preventing people from being victimized in the first place through the reform of society. Meanwhile, the agents of charity can dismiss justice advocates as refusing to get their hands dirty by working in direct service to the needy. Drawing the relationship of charity and justice that way is a terrible disservice to the Christian tradition.

The relationship of charity and justice is not one of opposition. There is a better way to think about these two virtues. In his social encyclical *Caritas in veritate*, Benedict XVI described the work of justice as the "institutional path—we might also call it the political path—of charity, no less excellent and effective than the kind of charity which encounters the neighbor directly." In other words, justice can be seen as the political expression of charity, or the application of charity to the institutional and structural aspects of a society.

Charity and justice are complementary and necessary moments in the response of Christians to the evils of poverty. Philanthropy and direct personal involvement are vitally important as disciples follow in the way of the Lord Jesus, but preventing further and future poverty through social reform is also a work of neighbor love. Indeed, it may be the only way that we can assist the distant neighbor whom we will not meet. The documents of Catholic social teaching make clear that the Christian tradition sets charity and justice not in tension but holds them up as dual obligations for those who hope to hear one day the words of Matthew 25:34–36: "Come, you that are blessed by my Father, inherit the kingdom prepared for you from the foundation of the world; for I was hungry and you gave me food, I was thirsty and you gave me something to drink, I was a stranger and you welcomed me, I was naked and you gave me clothing, I was sick and you took care of me, I was in prison and you visited me."

One

THE POOR
IN THE NEW TESTAMENT

BY PHEME PERKINS

In Matthew's Gospel, two familiar sayings about the poor serve as bookends to Jesus's public ministry. The Sermon on the Mount opens with the words "blessed are the poor in spirit, the Kingdom of heaven is theirs" (Matt. 5:3). As his public ministry concludes, Jesus is dining in the house of Simon, the leper, when an anonymous woman anoints his head with costly ointment (Matt. 26:6–13). Jesus rebukes his disciples who protest that it could have been sold and the money given to the poor with words that recall Deuteronomy 15:11, ". . . she has done a good deed for me, *for you always have the poor with you*, but you do not always have me." These key passages pose questions that bedevil any discussion of the poor in the New Testament. Insofar as New Testament writings insist on the ethical continuity between early Christian groups and their Jewish Scriptures, the social and legal understanding of how God's covenant people will treat the poor in their midst remain in force. Insofar as the figure of Jesus, not Torah observance, is the focal point of Christian piety, exemplary stories either about Jesus or told by him (parables) define how disciples should relate to the poor.

Who are the poor? The Greek word used in the New Testament refers to those who are in economic distress, the poor, the needy, the beggar, or otherwise dependent upon others. But as a Greek translation of various Hebrew terms in the Jewish Scriptures, the word extends from economic destitution to those in need of God's help (Ps. 82:3–4). That divine intervention to bring their distress to an end is announced as the "kingdom" or "reign" of God. Matthew's "poor *in spirit*" underlines this religious dimension without negating the economic meaning of the word.

Another Old Testament passage, which Jesus selects to introduce his ministry in Luke 4:17–19, is Isaiah 61:1–2. That text opens with preaching good news to the poor and includes healing those humbled in heart, and consoling those mourning, in addition to announcing freedom to prisoners, giving sight to the blind, and declaring the acceptable time (for debt relief) of the Lord. The initial group of beatitudes in Matthew 5:3–6 treats the sufferings of the poor, mourning, humble, hungering and thirsting for justice (righteousness) as reversed with the coming of God's Kingdom.

Over the past twenty-five years scholars have engaged in a lively debate over the question of the economic situation of believers in Jesus in Galilee as well as those comprising the urban house churches of the Pauline mission. Attempts to extrapolate from disparate and sparse archaeological and demographic data to produce a pattern of economic security and distress in urban communities have been more speculative than conclusive.

Neither the Jesus followers in Galilee nor the urban house churches of the Pauline mission had patrons from the wealthy, two percent of the aristocratic and governing elite. The majority probably belonged to those small farmers and urban tradesmen who were "poor" in the sense that their only reserves against a disaster were the social credit provided by family, trade associations in some cases, and the local community of friends and neighbors (1 Cor. 1:26–28). The destitute represented by street beggars, desperate day laborers, widows without family and the like constituted the bottom category in a poverty scale.

The New Testament views the rich, the top two to five percent of the scale, from the distance of those who ordinarily deal with such persons only through their various agents (for example, the unjust estate manager of Luke 16:1–8). Greedy and conspicuous consumption of wealth is excoriated (Luke 6:24–25; Jas. 5:1–6) because such persons do not employ the riches God provides to benefit those around them, as the Torah requires (see the parables of the Rich Fool, Luke 12:16–21, and the Rich Man and Lazarus, Luke 16:19–31).

Neither Jesus nor Paul has a socio-economic project for taking apart the structures of society in order to ". . . bring down the powerful . . . lift up the lowly; . . . fill the hungry with good things, and send the rich away empty . . ." (Luke 1:52–53). Only the final realization of God's reign at the end of days will accomplish that. No "war on poverty" is being declared in the Beatitudes. The moral imperative for God's people is to treat the poor, the disadvantaged, the resident alien, and the enslaved in their midst with justice because the God of Israel is the patron of such persons. This is both upheld and reinforced in the New Testament. It even creates new patterns of obligation, not common in the ancient world, when believers are asked to reach out to the "brothers and sisters" who are not part of their local community. Jesus imagines the "enemy" Samaritan as a better example of the Torah's love of neighbor to a Jewish victim than the priest and Levite who pass by (Luke 10:29–37). Paul asks Gentile believers from churches in Greece to provide material support for the poor Jewish Christians in Jerusalem by appealing to the example of Jesus as one who had renounced his own status in order to become poor (2 Cor. 8:9). Not only are the poor "always with you" as the neighbor in need, they are with us as those suffering poverty anywhere.

A dramatic example of this expanded concern to alleviate the suffering of any person, regardless of whether or not the individual is part of our social network, occurs in the final parable in Matthew's Gospel, the judgment separation of the sheep and the goats (Matt. 25:31–46). The only criterion for inclusion among those "blessed by my Father, to *inherit the Kingdom* prepared for you from the foundation of the world" (v. 34) is that those blessed provided food for the hungry, drink for the thirsty, welcome for the stranger, clothing for the naked, and visits (= assistance) to the sick and imprisoned. The mini-dialogue between Jesus, the judge, and the righteous and wicked respectively provides a fourfold repetition of the list. Like a musical refrain it should be etched in the memory of Matthew's audience. Commenting on this passage the great fifth-century preacher St. John Chrysostom pointed out to the congregation that Jesus did not ask them to work miracles and cure the sick or even to liberate prisoners, only to care for them. Surely an easy enough obligation (*Homily on Matthew* 79.1). But as long as God's Kingdom has not "come on earth as it is in heaven" (Matt. 6:10), these works of mercy remain daily chores in the household of faith.

The New Testament also provides examples in which even the requirements of charity toward the poor within the small house church communities was ignored. The Jewish Christian traditions preserved in the Epistle of James include "visiting the orphans and widows in their affliction" (1:27) in its definition of true religion. The term "visit" translates a Hebrew root that also means "watch over." It implies providing such persons with all possible loving protection and care. Only a few verses on, James denounces lapses in the community. The first involves partiality toward a rich person over the poor one in the assembly itself (2:1–13). "God has chosen the poor in the world to be rich in faith and *heirs to the Kingdom*, but you have dishonored the poor" (vv. 5–6). This condemnation echoes Matthew 5:3 and 25:34 as well as two passages from Proverbs in the Greek translation that was used by early Christians (Prov. 14:21, "one who dishonors the needy sins"). Some scholars think the situation in James involved a setting in which the community was to render judgment in a dispute rather than worship. Proverb 22:22, "do no violence to the needy for he is poor and do not dishonor the weak in the gates," concerns the legal standing of the poor. Then while challenging a misplaced Pauline slogan privileging faith over works, James insists that faith without the actual works of care for the poor is dead (2:15–26; also see 1 John 3:17). "If a brother or sister is naked and lacks daily food, and one of you says to them, 'Go in peace; keep warm and eat your fill,' and yet you do not supply their bodily needs, what good is that? So faith without works is dead" (vv. 15–17).

When Jesus says, "do not think I have come to abolish the law or the prophets . . . until heaven and earth pass away, not one letter, not one stroke of a letter will pass from the law . . ." in Matthew 5:17–18, he could have been referring to these works of mercy toward the poor. The poor certainly hunger and thirst to experience justice. But the eschatological "until heaven and earth pass away" also demands those virtues of endurance and hope. The poor are people, not a problem or project to be solved. Or as Jesus put it, "the least of these, my brothers."

Two

A DIFFICULT TEXT
"FOR YOU ALWAYS HAVE THE POOR WITH YOU"

BY BRUCE C. BIRCH AND LARRY RASMUSSEN

From: *Bible and Ethics in the Christian Life* (Minneapolis: Augsburg Fortress, 1976), 177–179.

Matthew 26:6–13 (see also Mark 14:3–9; John 12:1–8) tells of an incident in which a woman approaches Jesus and pours a jar of expensive ointment on his head. The disciples are scandalized by such waste and complain that money for the ointment could better have been given to the poor. Jesus intervenes by saying, "Why do you trouble the woman? For she has done a beautiful thing to me. For you always have the poor with you, but you will not always have me." He goes on to treat the anointing as a foreshadowing of his preparation for burial.

Jesus' statement, "For you always have the poor with you," has been a constant nemesis to those in the church who have tried to arouse the conscience of Christians to the harsh realities of poverty in our society and elsewhere in the world. Those who have defined the gospel solely in terms of individual and "internal" salvation use this text to justify a total lack of concern for the victims of poverty and the establishment of a just social order. They maintain that this text proclaims the futility of seeking to relieve the condition of the poor and focuses attention instead on the person of Jesus. To them this means the elevation of spiritual needs over material needs.

Indeed, if our exegesis is limited narrowly to this text we might well come to this point of view. Jesus *does* rebuke the disciples in their desire to give to the poor. He *does* turn attention to his own person. But does Jesus intend that we should not be concerned with the material needs of those who suffer? Is attention to Jesus' own person a turning to "spiritual" matters? When we move to a wider canonical context our understanding of this passage begins to alter.

The first move is naturally to the wider description of Jesus' ministry in the Gospels. From the very beginning Jesus identified his ministry with the poor and the oppressed. In Luke 4:16–19, at the inauguration of his public ministry, Jesus preaches at Nazareth and chooses as his text Isa. 61:1–2:

The Spirit of the Lord is upon me, because he has anointed me to preach good news to the poor. He has sent me to proclaim release to the captives and recovering of sight to the blind, to set at liberty those

*who are oppressed, to proclaim the acceptable year
of the Lord.*

Jesus associated himself with the poor and with society's
outcasts and was criticized for it (Matt. 11:19; Luke 7:34).
In his preaching, Jesus spoke with concern for the poor and
indicated that they were especially blessed by God (Luke
6:20–21). Perhaps most striking is the passage on the great
judgment in Matt. 25: 31–46:

*I was hungry and you gave me food, I was thirsty
and you gave me drink, I was a stranger and you
welcomed me, I was naked and you clothed me, I was
sick and you visited me, I was in prison and you came
to me.*

Jesus makes clear that his very person is identified with
the poor and the needy to the extent that acceptance of him
is equated with ministering to their needs. "Truly, I say to
you, as you did it to one of the least of these my brethren,
you did it to me" (Matt. 25:40).

In light of the strong witness elsewhere in the Gospels
to Jesus' concern with the material needs of the poor, we
surely cannot understand Jesus' statement in Matt. 26: 11
to be a repudiation of his own ministry. Jesus is focusing
attention in this passage on his own passion, but would not
be urging that we ignore the needs of the poor and needy.

Moving more widely in the canon we find in Deut. 15:7–11 a text with a statement so similar to that of Jesus that it raises the probability that Jesus is directly referring to it. This passage is a part of the law, the Torah, which was central to the faith of Jesus and the Jews of his time. The passage is making clear that concern for the poor is obligatory in the community of faith.

> *There will be no poor among you . . . if only you will obey the voice of the Lord your God. . . . If there is among you a poor man, one of your brethren, in any of your towns within your land which the Lord your God gives you, you shall not harden your heart or shut your hand against your poor brother, but you shall open your hand to him and lend him sufficient for his need. . . . You shall give to him freely, and your heart shall not be grudging. . . . For the poor will never cease out of the land; therefore, I command you, You shall open wide your hand to your brother, to the needy and to the poor. . . .*

This passage suggests that if the demands of the covenant were fully embodied there would be no poverty, but since Israel, like all human communities, is a "stiff-necked people," some of its inhabitants will inevitably be poor. Therefore, God's people are commanded to care for them. This task is part of what it means to be the people of God; it is not an optional activity.

This greatly alters our consideration of Matt. 26:6–13. Jesus is responding not to the disciples' desire to give to the poor, but to their rebuke of the woman. He is reminding them that the existence of the poor is a constant judgment against the whole covenant community. The woman is not to be self-righteously singled out; the poor are a corporate responsibility. By calling attention to the constant presence of the poor Jesus is not urging us to forget their needs. He is directly referring to God's command that we care for the poor, and their constant presence is an indictment pointing to our failure as the covenant community. It is because they are always present that we do have a responsibility. Jesus then goes on to use the woman's gift to focus attention on his own passion, his own ultimate involvement in human suffering.

A wider canonical context completely alters our view of this passage. If we had searched more broadly we would have found even more texts relating the people of God to the welfare of the poor (the prophets, Paul). Far from allowing anyone to narrowly interpret Matthew 26:6–13 as elevating spiritual over material needs, an exegesis in the context of the whole Scripture overwhelms us with the power of the moral imperative regarding the poor and needy.

Three

A SERMON ON LAZARUS AND THE RICH MAN

BY St. John Chrysostom

From: *On Wealth and Poverty*, trans. Catharine P. Roth (Yonkers, NY: St. Vladimir's Seminary Press, 1984), 40–41, 44, 45–47.

Let us learn from this man not to call the rich lucky nor the poor unfortunate. Rather, if we are to tell the truth, the rich man is not the one who has collected many possessions but the one who needs few possessions; and the poor man is not the one who has no possessions but the one who has many desires. We ought to consider this the definition of poverty and wealth. So if you see someone greedy for many things, you should consider him the poorest of all, even if he has acquired everyone's money. If, on the other hand, you see someone with few needs, you should count him the richest of all, even if he has acquired nothing. For we are accustomed to judge poverty and affluence by the disposition of the mind, not by the measure of one's substance.

Just as we would not call a person healthy who was always thirsty, even if he enjoyed abundance, even if he lived by rivers and springs (for what use is that luxuriance of water, when the thirst remains unquenchable?), let us do the same in the case of wealthy people: let us never consider those people healthy who are always yearning and thirsting after other people's property; let us not think that they enjoy any abundance. For if one cannot control his own greed, even if he has appropriated everyone's property, how can he ever be affluent? But those who are satisfied with what they have, and pleased with their own possessions, and do not have their eyes on the substance of others, even if they are the poorest of all, should be considered the richest of all. For whoever has no need of others' property but is happy to be self-sufficient is the most affluent of all. . . .

Are you listening to this in silence? I am much happier at your silence than at applause; for applause and praise make me more famous, but this silence makes you more virtuous. I know that what I say is painful, but I cannot tell you how great a benefit it contains. If that rich man had had someone to give him this kind of advice, instead of flatterers who always suggested what he wanted to hear, and who dragged him into luxurious living, he would not have fallen into that hell, nor undergone the unendurable torments, nor repented too late for consolation; but since they all made conversation for his pleasure, they handed him over to the fire. . . .

While we are here, we have good hopes; when we depart to that place, we have no longer the option of repentance, nor of washing away our misdeeds. For this reason we must continually make ourselves ready for our departure from here. What if the Lord wishes to call us this evening? Or tomorrow? The future is unknown, to keep us always active in the struggle and prepared for that removal, just as this Lazarus was patient in endurance. For this reason he was led away with such great honor. The rich man also died and was buried, just as his soul had lain buried in his body like a tomb, and had been wearing the flesh like a grave. For by shackling the flesh with drunkenness and gluttony as if with chains, he had made it useless and dead.

Do not simply pass over that phrase "he was buried," beloved: by it you should understand that the silver-inlaid tables, couches, rugs, tapestries, all other kinds of furnishings, sweet oils, perfumes, large quantities of undiluted wine, great varieties of food, rich dishes, cooks, flatterers, body-guards, household servants, and all the rest of his ostentation have been quenched and withered up. Now everything is ashes, all is dust and ashes, dirges and mourning, as no one is able to help any more, nor to bring back the soul which has departed. Then the power of gold is tested, and of all superfluous wealth. From such a crowd of attendants he was led away naked and alone, since he could not take anything with him out of such abundance; but he was led away without any companion or guide.

None of those who had attended him, none of those who had assisted him was able to save him from the punishment and retribution; but removed from all those followers, he was taken away alone to endure the unbearable retribution.

Truly, "All flesh is as the grass, and all the glory of mankind is as the flower of grass. The grass has withered, and its flower has faded; but the word of the Lord remains for ever." Death came and quenched all those luxuries; it took him like a captive and led him, hanging his head low, groaning with shame, unable to speak, trembling, afraid, as if he had enjoyed all that luxury in a dream.

Finally the rich man became a suppliant to the poor man and begged from the table of this man who earlier had gone hungry and been exposed to the mouths of dogs. The situation was reversed, and everyone learned who was really the rich man and was really the poor man, and that Lazarus was the most affluent of all but the other was the poorest of all. For just as on the stage actors enter with the masks of kings, generals, doctors, teachers, professors, and soldiers, without themselves being anything of the sort, so in the present life poverty and wealth are only masks. If you are sitting in the theater and see one of the actors wearing the mask of a king, you do not call him fortunate or think that he is a king, nor would you wish to become what he is; but since you know that he is some tradesman, perhaps a rope-maker or a coppersmith or something of the sort, you do not call him fortunate because of his mask and his costume, nor do you judge his social class by them, but reject this evidence because of the cheapness of his other garb. In the same way even here, sitting in this world as if in a theatre and looking at the players on the stage, when you see many rich people, do not think that they are truly rich, but that they are wearing the masks of rich people. Just as that man who acts the part of king or general on the stage often turns out to be a household servant or somebody who sells figs or grapes in the market, so also the rich man often turns out to be the poorest of all. If you take off his mask, open up his conscience, and enter into his mind, you will often find there a great poverty of virtue: you will find that he belongs to the lowest class of all.

Just as in the theater, when evening falls and the audience departs, and the kings and generals go outside to remove the costumes of their roles, they are revealed to everyone thereafter appearing to be exactly what they are; so also now when death arrives and the theater is dissolved, everyone puts off the masks of wealth or poverty and departs to the other world. When all are judged by their deeds alone, some are revealed truly wealthy, others poor, some of high class, others of no account.

Often indeed one of those who are rich in this life turns out to be the poorest of all in the other life, even like this rich man. For when the evening took him, that is to say death, and he departed from the theater of the present life, and put aside his mask he was revealed as the poorest of all in that other world; so poor indeed that he was not master even of a drop of water, but had to beg for this and did not even obtain it by begging. What could be poorer than this poverty?

Four

A VOW OF POVERTY

BY SANDRA MARIE SCHNEIDERS, IHM

From: *New Wineskins: Re-imaging Religious Life Today*
(Mahwah, NJ: Paulist Press, 1986), 178–190.

The proper understanding and prudent practice of religious poverty has probably never been easy in any age. It is of the very nature of religious poverty, because it has to do with material goods with which we cannot dispense absolutely and whose value is always relative to cultural situations, that it is always a provisional arrangement that has to be constantly re-evaluated and readjusted.

Our own times are characterized by conditions that make the understanding and prudent practice of poverty even more difficult than in times past. The major difference between our own age and any previous one, in relation to poverty, is our global interdependence at the economic level and our awareness of it.

First, we are aware of the immense variety in standards of living throughout the world and even in our own country. No matter how simple a lifestyle we adopt we cannot escape awareness that it is luxurious by comparison with that of many of our sisters and brothers. . . .

Second, we are aware of the immensity of the problem of poverty which makes individual acts of sharing and hospitality seem almost pointless. . . .

Third, and following from the last point, we realize that the only way to affect the economic situation in which we live is to act collectively upon institutions. Poverty, the evil which is eating up our brothers and sisters in so many places in the world, is not natural disaster nor merely the result of individual selfish choices. It is a systemic evil that must be dealt with systematically; it is institutional sin that must be dealt with institutionally. Whatever poverty means today, it has to take account of these realities.

THE TWO FOCI OF RELIGIOUS POVERTY TODAY

Religious poverty has two foci for the contemporary religious and calls for two rather distinct, though not unrelated, types of practice. The first focus is the societal one and has to do with our individual and corporate impact on the institutional sins which are making and keeping poor the majority of the earth's people while the minority becomes progressively richer. The second focus is the personal spiritual one which has to do with our own ascetical preparation for and interior exercise of that openness to God in grateful receptivity to salvation that is the sine qua non of genuine holiness.

1. *The Societal Focus.* Religious poverty is the way religious situate themselves in relationship to material goods, and since material goods are foundational to our relationship with other people, religious poverty is necessarily a social virtue. . . . It seems to me, and to many religious, that the first objective of religious poverty today has to be contributing to the restructuring of the economic situation on a worldwide scale. This seems especially so for apostolic religious for whom the call to participate actively in the transformation of the world in Christ is so integral to their religious vocation.

There are innumerable ways in which religious can begin to exercise their vow of poverty in relation to the economic and environmental situation of our time. . . . The energetic exercise of *personal civic responsibilities* such as voting, writing to congress people, protesting local injustices, supporting non-violent efforts to influence corporate powers, attending meetings where our presence can help, is a way to help bring about the kind of society in which the poor will begin to attain justice.

Proper *corporate planning for the care of our own personnel* is another unglamorous but important contribution to the future well-being of our society. As a society we are getting older. We can plan for a future in which the elderly will have secure, meaningful, and productive lives or we can ignore the demographic data available to us and let develop a world of underemployed, unfulfilled people dragging out meaningless existences in a world that does not want them.

Another important area of personal and corporate decision making concerns the appropriate and effective *commitment of some of our personnel and resources to direct work with the materially disadvantaged*. For some of us it will be the decision to undertake that work ourselves; for others the decision to support those who do in one way or another.

Direct *involvement in political ministry* . . . is a particularly powerful way to influence the distribution of money and services to the poor.

This certainly does not exhaust the possibilities of active involvement in the restructuring of our world in justice and love. These are meant only to suggest that the vow of poverty today calls upon us to do for our time what our forebears did in simpler and more direct ways for theirs.

2. *The Personal Focus*. It is perhaps time to revive our awareness of the intimately personal character of the practice of poverty which must complement societal involvement. . . . Without even hoping to exhaust the possibilities I would like to point out, by way of example, a few areas in which the incorporation of poverty into our personal lives might be meaningful and spiritually fruitful for us as twentieth century religious.

The first area is one most serious religious have been bewitched, bothered, and bewildered by for several years: *simplicity of life.* . . . Voluntary simplicity of lifestyle says that enough is enough, that material goods should be acquired only to the extent that they are really necessary and not as a frantic defense against mortality or an endless competition with one's neighbors.

But simplicity of life also fulfills an important function in the spiritual life of the individual. . . . If we want to pray, to be available for God and others, to keep our lives focused on the purposes for which we chose religious life, we cannot surrender ourselves to the current of materialism that carries our culture.

A second area in which poverty might touch our personal lives has to do less with behavior than with attitude. I am speaking of the deliberate development of the *sense of gift in life.* We live in a culture of achievement and production which believes that people should and do get what they deserve. As Christians we know that this is not so. The infinite bounty of God begins with the gift of life itself and continues with everything that sustains it. Our activity is not so much an earning our way as a cooperating with the Creator God in transforming history into God's reign of justice and love. Building this attitude of grateful response into our lives requires a constant cultivation of faith against the seemingly self-evident "way things are" around us. . . . The capacity for enjoyment, for the sharing of simple pleasures, for delight in uncontrived beauty, has to be developed in our artificial and overstimulated environment.

A third area in which the personal practice of poverty might be developed today is one that was not available to many religious in more enclosed times: *hospitality*. To welcome others into our homes and into our lives is naturally easier perhaps for extroverted types, but it is a challenge for everyone because it involves putting ourselves at others' disposal.

Another area of personal poverty, one that seems to me more and more significant, has to do with one of the most painful aspects of real poverty, namely, the *lack of options*. The real differences between the truly poor and people who choose a poor lifestyle is precisely that the latter choose it, and they can unchoose it if things become too difficult. Even if they never do, the fact that they can assuages the violent determinism that constitutes real poverty. . . .

There are many aspects of our lives in which we have choices that the poor do not have. But there are also areas in which we do not have choices. We cannot lengthen our day, and if someone consumes time we had allotted for other purposes there is no reclaiming it. We cannot do anything about weather that keeps us from getting where we need to go. We cannot keep from getting the flu and losing a week of work at a critical juncture in an important project. . . . When our options evaporate we experience solidarity with the poor, not the conspicuous solidarity of chosen deprivations but the real solidarity of fellow-sufferers in a world we do not control and cannot change.

One of the many areas in which many of us probably experience our lack of options most painfully is precisely that of effective action for justice. We know that most of what we do, in a personal way, will not have much effect on the unjust social systems in which we live. Even worse, we also know that we are constantly implicated in fostering the very systems that we have analyzed as unjust and exploitative. . . . The point is, in many areas we really have few or no options either for effective action against or for non-participation in structural injustice. Our frustration matches in some ways (certainly not all) the frustration of our victimized brothers and sisters. What they cannot do for themselves we cannot do for them, and the more we care the more this hurts. The name of that hurting is compassion and it is a fruit of genuine poverty.

CONCLUSION

Let me conclude with a simple, tentative definition of religious poverty. Religious poverty is an evangelically inspired and structured relationship to material creation which involves owning well, using well, and suffering well for the purpose of transforming human existence, our own included. Its goal is a community in which all have the material supports necessary for truly human living whose fullest realization is that total openness to God which makes salvation possible and real.

Five

I'M NOT ANGRY SO MUCH AS I'M REALLY TIRED

BY LINDA TIRADO

Excerpts from one chapter titled, "I'm Not Angry So Much as I'm Really Tired," in *Hand to Mouth: Living in Bootstrap America* by Linda Tirado (New York: G. P. Putnam's Sons, 2014), 54, 56–57, 57–58, 61–63, 67, 70, 74–76, 76–77, 78.

Often enough, I *feel* less than human—or less than the human that I know myself to be. For example, I love to read. I'm a naturally curious person, apt to ask uncomfortable questions without realizing it because I just want to know something. But I don't read when I'm working at minimum wage or near it. I'm too tired. I fall asleep because the effort of moving my eyes across the page and processing information is simply too much; my brain won't allow me to use what little energy I have left on frivolities like self-improvement. It just wants me to stare blankly at a wall or flickering screen until I pass out. . . .

When some wealthier people sense an unwillingness in lower-paid workers to move faster than they absolutely have to, or to do much of anything with their free time, it's because we are marshalling our resources. We're not lazy, we're stockpiling our leisure while we can. I can't tolerate more mental exercise after a full day of logistics and worry. Full capacity isn't an option.

We start the day with a deficit. . . . [P]oor people wake up knowing that today, no matter how physically [poor] we may feel, we can't call in sick or slack off at our desk surfing the Internet. We have to go to our crappy jobs no matter what. We will feel guilty about the bills and the dishes and we will firmly put them out of our mind as we march out the door in our polyester uniform shirts. . . .

Regardless of our mood, we're never fully checked into work because our brains are taken up with at least one and sometimes all of the following: 1) calculating how much we'll make if we stay an extra hour, 2) worrying we'll be sent home early because it's slow and theorizing how much we will therefore lose, 3) placing bets on whether we will be allowed to leave in time to make it to our other job or pick up our kids. Meanwhile, we spend massive amounts of energy holding down the urge to punch something after the last customer called us an idiot. People don't have any compunction about insulting service workers, but it's amazing how quickly they'll complain about your attitude if you're not sufficiently good natured about it.

Our jobs are as much emotional labor as they are physical. What they are not, what they are never allowed to be, is mentally engaging. So we're trying to zombie out to survive. We're not allowed to deviate from policy even if the policy is kind of stupid and counterproductive. Nobody is interested in our thoughts, opinions, or the contributions we might be able to make—they want robots.

Our survival mechanisms are the things that annoy the customers most. Next time you see someone being "sullen" or "rude," try being nice to them. It's likely you'll be the first person to do so in hours. Alternatively, ask them an intelligent question. I used to come alive when someone legitimately wanted to know what I'd recommend. I knew everything about my products, having stared at all the boxes while I restocked them, but people rarely wanted me to tell them anything more about the price.

What's guaranteed to be counterproductive for you is demanding better service. We'll perform better service. But we'll be sure to hand you the shirt that we know is stained, or the meat that's within the technical limit of servable but will probably taste less than optimal. And we'll do it with a [stupid] grin on our face and well-wishes on our lips, just like you demand but refuse to pay a single extra penny for.

If you want us to be happy to serve you, make it worth our while and be pleasant. Next time you're in a low wage place, try walking up to an employee and saying, "I'm sorry to disturb you, I know you have work, but could you tell me where this thing I need is?" I guarantee you, *that* is how you get service from a demoralized staff. Respect their workload. There is no low-wage employer in the world that doesn't expect a ton of chores finished in a shift besides customer service. Don't just expect that millions of people are by nature pleased to grovel at the feet of your twenty dollars. Humans in general aren't built that way. . . .

I recognize that the [rough] attitude that I [and some other low-wage workers] fall into . . . as a ward against the instability of being poor isn't always helpful to me. But it's not as if I can just go in and out of it, like putting on or taking off my makeup. The attitude I carry as a poor person is my armor, and after so many years of fighting and clawing and protecting myself and my family from impending disaster, that armor has become a permanent part of me. . . .

[For example,] I walk with a tiny swagger. Many people who have lived in the not-so-nice parts of cities do this to varying degrees because it tells people from a distance that we know how to handle ourselves, and that we are streetwise enough to make a challenging target. It's also unconscious in me at this point. To middle- and upper-class people, it's one more thing that sets me apart, that sends the unintended signal that I don't belong in nicer company. . . .

I didn't really realize that I was fully lower class in both sensibilities and presentation until I found myself at what was the last of my professional social engagements. I was attempting to resurrect something like a career during the worst part of our stay in Ohio, when we weren't getting our GI Bill stipend, and I thought maybe I could scrape something up. I was invited out to dinner by a bunch of old political work colleagues, and I found myself with nothing to say. I had no insights on the new restaurants or movies or bars, nothing that you typically reach for to make conversation. Every single addition I could have made would have been inappropriate: I couldn't have talked about my neighbor getting in a fight with his truck while he was drunk because it wouldn't start and he thought punching it might help. (His roommate had disabled the thing. Friends don't let friends drink and drive, and smart friends let friends punch trucks instead of them.) I couldn't talk about which food banks were best for produce and which for diapers. I also didn't order any food or drinks, which was pointed out repeatedly by the waiter. ("Are you *sure* you won't be ordering? Can I tempt you with this/that/the other?") I finally had to leave the table, track him down, explain that I couldn't afford anything on the menu, and ask could he *please* stop making a huge deal out of it? After that, I never called any of those colleagues again. Nor did they call me.

I understand why this happened. But what I don't understand is why people who walk into a fast-food restaurant often seem to think I should put on the same smile and elegant demeanor they could expect at Saks or the bank where they put their money. I think that the sorts of people who think service workers should be more smiley and gracious just don't get it. They don't get it because they can take so much for granted in their own lives— things like respect, consideration, and basic fairness on the job. Benefits. Insurance. . . . They don't understand how depressing it is to be barely managing your life at any given moment of the day. So forgive me if I don't tell you to have a pleasant day with unfeigned enthusiasm when I hand you your [food]. You'll have to settle for the fake sort. . . .

[Work is] what we spend a huge percentage of our lives on. And how we're treated there isn't something we can just shake off when we leave. It becomes a part of us, just like that armor we wear.

But still we're told to keep smiling, and to be grateful for the chance to barely survive while being blamed for not succeeding. Whether or not that's actually true isn't even relevant; that's what it feels like. Unwinnable. Sisyphean. . . .

So that's been my American dream. And it's reality for millions of us, the people who are looking grumpy behind the counter. Our bodies hurt, our brains hurt, and our souls hurt. There's rarely anything to smile about.

Six

DISPLACEMENT AS A FORM OF POVERTY

BY HENRI J. NOUWEN, DONALD P. MCNEILL, CSC, AND DOUGLAS A. MORRISON

From: *Compassion: A Reflection on the Christian Life* (New York: Knopf Doubleday, 2005), 60–73.

According to Webster's dictionary, displacement means, to move or to shift from the ordinary or proper place. This becomes a telling definition when we realize the extent to which we are preoccupied with adapting ourselves to the prevalent norms and values of our milieu. We want to be ordinary and proper people who live ordinary and proper lives. There is an enormous pressure on us to do what is ordinary and proper—even the attempt to excel is ordinary and proper—and thus find the satisfaction of general acceptance.

The call to community as we hear it from our Lord is the call to move away from the ordinary and proper places. Leave your father and mother. Let the dead bury the dead. Keep your hand on the plow and do not look back. Sell what you own. Give the money to the poor and come follow me

(Lk 14:26; 9:60, 62; 18:22). The Gospels confront us with this persistent voice inviting us to move from where it is comfortable, from where we want to stay, from where we feel at home.

Why is this so central? It is central because in voluntary displacement, we cast off the illusion of "having it together" and thus begin to experience our true condition, which is that we, like everyone else, are pilgrims on the way, sinners in need of grace. Through voluntary displacement we counteract the tendency to become settled in a false comfort and to forget the fundamentally unsettled position that we share with all people. Voluntary displacement leads us to the existential recognition of our inner brokenness and thus brings us to a deeper solidarity with the brokenness of our fellow human beings.

FOLLOWING THE DISPLACED LORD

Voluntary displacement as a way of life rather than as a unique event is the mark of discipleship. Jesus, whose compassion we want to manifest in time and place, is indeed displaced. Paul describes Jesus as the one who voluntarily displaced himself. "His state was divine, yet he did not cling to his equality with God but emptied himself to assume the condition of a slave, and became as we are" (Ph 2:6–7). A greater displacement cannot be conceived. The mystery of the incarnation is that God did not remain in the place that we consider proper for God but moved to the condition of a suffering human being. God *gave up* the heavenly place and took a humble place among mortal men and women. God became displaced so that nothing human would be alien and the brokenness of our human condition could be fully experienced.

Jesus Christ is the displaced Lord in whom God's compassion becomes flesh. In him, we see a life of displacement lived to the fullest. It is in following our displaced Lord that the Christian community is formed. Jesus' call to voluntary displacement has a very contemporary ring. It is obviously not a call to disruptive behavior, but a call to solidarity with the millions who live disrupted lives.

It is worth noting the great role voluntary displacement has played in the history of Christianity. Benedict went to Subiaco, Francis to the Carceri, Ignatius to Manresa, Charles de Foucauld to the Sahara, John Wesley to the poor districts in England, Mother Teresa to Calcutta, and Dorothy Day to the Bowery. With their followers, they moved from the ordinary and proper places to the places where they could experience and express their compassionate solidarity with those in whom the brokenness of the human condition was most visible. We can indeed say that voluntary displacement stands at the origin of all great religious reforms.

ST. FRANCIS OF ASSISI

The most inspiring and challenging example of displacement is St. Francis of Assisi. In 1209, this son of a wealthy merchant tore his clothes from his body and walked away from his family and friends to live a life of abject poverty. By moving naked out of the fortified city with its power and security and by living in caves and in the open fields, Francis called attention to the basic poverty of humanity. He revealed not only his own nakedness but also the nakedness of all people before God. From this displaced position, Francis could live a compassionate life; he was no longer blinded by apparent differences between people and could recognize them all as brothers and sisters who needed God's grace as much as he did. G. K. Chesterton writes:

> What gave him extraordinary personal power was this; that from the Pope to the beggar, from the Sultan of Syria in his pavilion to the ragged robbers crawling out of the wood, there was never a man who looked into those brown burning eyes without being certain that Francis Bernardone was really interested in him, in his own inner individual life from the cradle to the grave; that he himself was being valued and taken seriously, and not merely added to the spoils of some social policy or the names in some clerical document. . . . He treated the whole mob of men as a mob of Kings.[1]

In the small group of brothers who followed Francis in his poverty, the compassionate life was lived. These men, who had nothing to share but their poverty and who made themselves fully dependent on God's grace, formed a genuine fellowship of the weak in which they could live together in compassion and extend their compassion to all whom they met on the road. Their communal life of poverty prepared them for unlimited compassion.

St. Francis offers us an impressive example of displacement that leads to community and compassion. By moving away from their "ordinary and proper places," St. Francis and his followers illuminated the oneness of the human race. They did this not only by the way they lived together but also by the way they created space for others in their common life.

The history of the Franciscans, however, also illustrates that as soon as success and wealth seduce people back to their ordinary and proper places, community as well as compassion is hard to find. This was not only true for the Franciscans but also for many other religious groups as well. It is therefore understandable that the history of Christianity is filled with reformers who constantly displace themselves to remind us of our great vocation to a compassionate life.

If we really want to be compassionate people, it is urgent that we reclaim this great tradition of displacement. As long as our houses, parishes, convents, and monasteries are only ordinary and proper places, they will only awaken ordinary and proper responses and nothing will happen. As long as religious people are well dressed, well fed, and well cared for, words about being in solidarity with the poor will remain pious words more likely to evoke good feelings than creative actions. As long as we are only doing well what others are doing better and more efficiently, we can hardly expect to be considered the salt of the earth or the light of the world. In short, as long as we avoid displacement, we will miss the compassionate life to which Jesus calls us.

Not everyone is called in the way St. Francis, Dorothy Day, Mother Teresa, and Jean Vanier were called. But everyone must live with the deep conviction that God acts in her or his life in an equally unique way. No one should ever think that he or she is just an "ordinary citizen" in the Reign of God. As soon as we start taking ourselves and God seriously and allow him to enter into a dialogue with us, we will discover that we also are asked to leave fathers, mothers, brothers, and sisters to follow Jesus in obedience. Quite often we will discover that we are asked to follow to places we would rather not go. But when we have learned to respond to the small displacements of our daily lives, the greater call will not seem so great after all. We then will find the courage to follow him and be amazed by our freedom to do so.

Thus, voluntary displacement is a part of the life of each Christian. It leads away from the ordinary and proper places, whether this is noticed by others or not; it leads to a recognition of each other as fellow travelers on the road, and thus creates community. Finally, voluntary displacement leads to compassion; by bringing us closer to our own brokenness it opens our eyes to our fellow human beings, who seek our consolation and comfort.

Seven

THE STRUCTURAL PROBLEM OF WORKING POVERTY

BY CONOR M. KELLY

One sobering element of poverty in the United States is the phenomenon of the working poor. This category includes individuals and families whose income from employment is not enough to meet their basic needs. Contrary to stereotypes of "the poor" as a monolithic group of people whose individual choices have made them destitute, the existence of the working poor in the United States reveals that poverty is a multifaceted, structural problem. Consequently, the Catholic response must be multifaceted and structural as well.

A little bit of basic arithmetic illustrates the reality of working poverty. The federal minimum wage is currently set at $7.25 per hour, which translates to an annual pretax income of $15,080—assuming one works full time and has no unpaid sick or vacation days. This income is enough to exceed the Census Bureau's poverty threshold for a single adult living alone, but if a worker has even one child at home, then his or her income from a *full-time* job will fall $1,237 short of the poverty threshold. For single parents raising two children on the income from a minimum wage job, their household will be $3,993 short of the poverty threshold, which means they would need to earn more than 125 percent of their regular wage (about $9.17 per hour) merely to meet the poverty threshold.[2]

As bad as these numbers are, they still only reveal part of the story. First, most low-wage jobs in the current economy are not full-time jobs, so translating a minimum wage job, or even one paying more than the minimum wage, into a yearly income of $15,080 is no easy feat. Taking these difficulties into account, the Census Bureau estimates that 10.6 million people were members of the working poor in 2012. This was just over seven percent of the U.S. workforce and nearly a quarter of all individuals living in poverty.[3] As such, the working poor is a bigger group than the minimum wage arithmetic might suggest.

Second, even these statistics are understated because the federal poverty benchmarks are notoriously low. Today's thresholds are an inflation-adjusted version of a 1963 assessment of poverty, which was determined by tripling the minimum cost of food for a family. At the time, this was a reasonable assumption, since most families spent approximately one third of their income on food. Today, however, when health care and housing represent much larger portions of a family's typical expenditures, the same methodology misrepresents the problem.[4] Thus, while almost 11 million people are officially classified as part of the working poor, the reality is that even more people are unable to make ends meet despite their workforce participation.

The large number of individuals who remain in poverty while working is indicative of a serious problem with the nature of work in the United States. From a Catholic perspective, this problem is almost self-evident. According to the Church's social doctrine, "work is a fundamental dimension of human existence on earth," and the innate dignity of the human person gives an inherent value to his or her work as well.[5] The Church therefore insists, "the basis for determining the value of human work is not primarily the kind of work being done but the fact that the one who is doing it is a person."[6] One should not be surprised, then, that the first social encyclical, *Rerum Novarum*, proclaimed that "wages ought not to be insufficient to support a frugal and well-behaved wage earner."[7] The existence of the working poor directly contradicts this basic tenet of Catholic social teaching.

The fact that a "frugal and well-behaved wage earner" can work full time and fail to support herself or himself—let alone a family—is a clear indication that work is undervalued. This should not just be a Catholic conclusion, but an objective one as well. The problem is most evident at the lower end of the wage scale, but it can also be seen in the persistent stagnation of wages that is beginning to affect all but the highest echelons of the U.S. economy. Put simply, workers in the United States are not reaping the benefits of their labor, for even as the recovery from the Great Recession gains speed, remuneration for work is all but unchanged.

The causes of our current period of wage stagnation are frequently contested, but the structural roots behind this issue become more apparent when one takes a broader view. In actuality, wage stagnation is not a post-Recession occurrence but a thirty-year reality. Since the late 1970s, wages have fallen in real (i.e., inflation-adjusted) terms for 60 percent of workers, and average wages for all workers increased a meager 0.2 percent between 1979 and 2011. The structural injustice is evident in the fact that during the same period, workers' economic output increased almost 70 percent, yet their total compensation (including all wages and benefits) improved only 7 percent. Contrast this situation with the period immediately following World War II, when productivity increased 254 percent and hourly compensation increased 113 percent.[8] In other words, whereas our society once saw it fit to distribute one half of the improvements in economic performance to workers, today we are only willing to reward them with only one tenth of those gains.

The split between productivity and workers' compensation is largely due to shifts in the way businesses are run in this country. Prior to the 1970s, most companies assumed that their continued success required training and retaining qualified workers, so profits were broadly distributed throughout a corporation's workforce. As global competition increased, however, workers became liabilities on the financial statement, and many companies looked to increase profits instantly by laying off large portions of their workforce. This decision was typically rewarded by investors, many of whom were more focused on short-term returns rather than long-term prospects. The result was a spate of layoffs, first in manufacturing and then in management, during the 1970s and 1980s, which led to higher unemployment and lower wages as the supply of workers exceeded demand.[9]

This history is important because it illustrates that the existence of the working poor is very much a systemic injustice found in the structures of the U.S. economy. It is also valuable because a more accurate diagnosis can help the people of God better determine adequate responses to the challenges of the working poor.

One response is simple: pay higher wages. The Catholic Church has long supported the right of workers to receive a "living wage" as a form of just remuneration for their labors. The exact definition of this term is frequently debated, but the idea is to ensure that those who work full time have a sufficient amount of income from their jobs to allow them to support themselves and, in the Catholic assessment, their families. Thus, the living wage movement in the United States promotes slogans such as, "A job should lift you out of poverty, not keep you in it," and sets its living wage benchmark as the hourly wage that would lift a family of four above the federal poverty threshold.[10]

The threshold for a family of four is a good benchmark because it accounts for the underinflated nature of the federal poverty thresholds, and because it also respects the right of a worker to provide for his or her dependents, something Catholic Social Teaching and Catholic theologians have long championed.[11] Assuming full-time employment for 50 weeks a year (granting a little bit of sick time and vacation time), this would equate to a $12 per hour wage rate. If Catholics are serious about addressing the problem of the working poor, they ought to champion raising the minimum wage to this level.

Admittedly, changing national policy is a lofty goal, and it will take time, so the Church as a whole, and individual Catholics on their own, should also seek ways to advance the progressive realization of higher wages on a more immediate basis. For those Catholics who own businesses or otherwise supervise employees, they can make a concerted effort to ensure that their workers earn living wages. This could result from a unilateral decision to raise wages, but it would likely be more sustainable if Catholic employers followed the example of Reell Precision Manufacturing, which hired workers at the market rate but committed to training all new employees until their productivity levels could offset a living wage. Certainly, this is a model to which Catholic parishes, schools, hospitals, and universities ought to commit themselves.

For those Catholics who do not own businesses, they can still effect positive changes with their financial decisions. After all, consumers are among the biggest beneficiaries of low labor costs, so it is only fair that we should make some sacrifices to restore a more just valuation of work. Catholics should therefore become conscientious consumers, intentionally spending our dollars at businesses known for good labor practices and vocally avoiding notorious violators of workers' rights.

Ultimately, these small changes could help to reduce the prevalence of working poverty, but given the structural roots of this problem, even support for living wages will not be enough. For real changes to occur, the structure of remuneration for labor will have to change, otherwise the benefits of increases in productivity will never go to the workers themselves and ever-greater disparities will exacerbate the challenges of the poor in our society.

One structural alternative is worker cooperatives. In these businesses, the employees are the shareholders and vice versa, so there is no conflict between improving employment conditions and maximizing shareholder value. The result is a much more equitable distribution of a company's profits because cooperatives do not pay stock dividends; instead, they turn increased profits into higher wages for everyone, from the newest worker to the most seasoned manager.[12] Moreover, cooperatives are also more likely to weather economic downturns together, temporarily instituting universal pay cuts in order to minimize layoffs, thereby further undermining the business models that contribute to working poverty.[13]

Not every company can form a worker cooperative, but that does not mean they are excused from responding to the plight of the working poor. There are other alternatives to the current economic structures that make working poverty a reality, and a creative person at any company can almost certainly find a model that would work for her or his employer. In these efforts in particular, Catholics ought to apply themselves with a special vigor so that they can provide a prophetic witness. If done well, the Church can thereby testify that sustainable business models can respect the dignity of work and of workers, and that economies do not need to assume the existence of the working poor in order to survive. This will certainly not eliminate poverty, but if we can at least reduce the numbers of the working poor, we will have taken a major step in the right direction.

Eight

THE POOR AND THE ENVIRONMENT

BY MICHAEL MUTZNER AND ALESSANDRA AULA

From: *World Poverty: Franciscan Reflections* (Geneva: Franciscans International, 2007), 186–189.

At its core, poverty results from the lack of access to the resources necessary for a life of dignity. Improving wages and providing an adequate social safety net are fundamental components of poverty eradication, but economic income alone does not guarantee freedom from poverty. Addressing the sum total of environmental conditions may be required as well. Tackling air pollution, inadequate water infrastructure, and insufficient housing stock are social justice issues, but also issues of human ecology. For example, in California's Central Valley, these problems are exacerbated by racism and anti-immigrant bias, all within an hour's drive from some of the wealthiest cities in the world. California needs a sustainable development strategy just as much as Africa. Here we suffer from over-development, or mal development: tremendous economic growth has benefited many, but millions have been left behind in this economy. The poor are further marginalised as environmental resources are exploited for the privileged, but air quality deteriorates, providing a further injustice. Human society does need to exploit environmental resources to support itself, but the distribution of pollutants and the degradation of resources usually impacts the poor much more heavily. From a Christian perspective, the poor also have a right to development, but our advocacy must be very clear: it must be an equitable, sustainable development, at both regional and international scales.

THE EMERGENCE OF A CATHOLIC ETHIC OF ENVIRONMENTAL JUSTICE

St. Francis of Assisi was named patron saint of those who "promote ecology" by Pope John Paul II in 1979. 1 Despite a widely held popular perception of St. Francis as a model for environmental advocacy, the Franciscan Family has committed astonishingly few resources to this critical task. Analysing and correcting this shortcoming in Franciscan praxis is beyond the scope of this chapter, but we do feel it is important to provide some theological foundation for an integrated approach to advocating for the poor and the environment. With his 1990 World Day of Peace Message Pope John Paul II launched a flurry of interest in environmental matters among Catholic theologians. John Paul II rooted his environmental theology in the stewardship ethic of Genesis, and linked it with his vision for solidarity with the poorest on this planet. He carried forward a goal for distributive justice of the earth's resources for everyone, initiated by Pope Leo XII in *Rerum Novarum* (1891) and affirmed by the major statements of Catholic social teaching for the past century. More than anyone else, Pope John Paul II conferred legitimacy on Catholic concern for the environment.

The power of capitalism and technology has made unprecedented resource exploitation possible. In North America, conventional environmentalism and popular perceptions have posed environmental protection (especially wild areas and habitat) to be in tension with economic development. Media narratives and popular perception recount how resource exploitation and pollution are inevitable consequences of job creation and economic growth. Over the past twenty years, however, an alternative approach has emerged, linking social justice and environmental protection. Its advocates carry forward a progressive agenda from the civil rights, labor rights, and community organizing movements. This approach critiques conventional environmentalism as reproducing the discrimination of broader US society, and failing to acknowledge the disproportionate impact of pollution on economically and politically marginalized communities. Frequently these are communities of color, already suffering from poor housing, failing schools, and inadequate job opportunities. A disproportionate burden of pollution adds further injury to the injustice they suffer. To emphasize the centrality of equity issues in this agenda, movement leaders named their approach Environmental Justice.

The Environmental Justice movement grew out of these other historical social movements for justice, and its integrated vision grew as scholars began to describe the common patterns of injustice suffered by inner city African Americans, Native Americans on reservations, and rural Mexican Americans (especially farmworkers and rural communities). During the 1980s and 1990s, the movement focused most of its efforts on local, urban initiatives to address toxic waste disposal and workplace hazards (including pesticides). Scholars played a critical role in framing these local initiatives as a national movement, and some Protestant churches conferred legitimacy, especially the United Church of Christ and African American congregations that had been active in civil rights efforts. By the mid-1990s, the Environmental Justice movement had established its alternative environmental agenda with an explicit focus on the needs of poor communities. Several scholars have subsequently expanded the EJ framework to an international scale.

Pope John Paul II's World Day of Peace message was substantially echoed by the US Bishops' conference in 1991 with their Renewing the Earth: An Invitation to Reflection and Action on Environment in Light of Catholic Social

Teaching. Coming just five years after their major economic justice pastoral letter, the US Bishops presented their vision of a distinctly Catholic contribution to environmental concerns. In keeping with John Paul's vision, the document presents Biblical and sacramental visions of stewardship, reflecting a Biblical vision of justice. More than other statements, it emphasises continuity between economic justice and environmental justice, meaning solidarity with the economically marginalized who suffer disproportionate environmental impacts. Renewing the Earth proposed a distinct Catholic environmental ethic, drawn from the Church's social teaching tradition. It lays out familiar social teaching themes from which to fashion an environmental ethic: a sacramental universe, a consistent respect for human life, common good, solidarity, universal purpose of created things, and an option for the poor. By 1996, forty-eight conferences of bishops worldwide had written statements addressing specific, regional environmental problems from the perspective of Catholic theology, with a special emphasis on just distribution of resources for the poor.

At the national level, the US Bishops established an environmental justice program to assist parishes and dioceses who wanted to conduct education, outreach, and advocacy about these issues. The most interesting and effective expressions of Catholic environmental justice concern have been regional initiatives. These have quite deliberately integrated economic development, distributive justice, and common good concerns. US Bishops do not want Catholic environmental concern to be perceived as distinct or deviating from their broader strategy of presenting social teaching to the faithful and society.

These regional initiatives assume greater power because they apply social teaching principles to specific economic and environmental conditions, and because they facilitate participation by concerned lay Catholics. In 1996, the Catholic Bishops of Appalachia wrote *At Home in the Web of Life* to propose the creation and defense of "sustainable communities" as a task for the Catholics and people of this region. Appalachia has long been treated as a resource colony, and this letter proposes a vision of sustainable forests, agriculture, families, livelihoods, spirituality, and communities.

The best known regional environmental pastoral letter was created by the bishops of the Pacific Northwest, British Columbia, and Alberta in 2001, *The Columbia River Watershed: Caring for Creation and the Common Good*. These bishops banded together based on the region surrounding the Columbia River. Their letter proposes a ten-point action plan, including the promotion of justice for the poor, linking economic justice and environmental justice.

Several other regions of bishops have issued shorter and less ambitious pastoral letters on the environment, usually re-stating core Catholic social teaching principles as they apply to environmental concerns. Common themes include a call for better stewardship of the earth, more authentic models of economic development, and attention to the crisis in agriculture and rural communities.

Nine

POVERTY QUIZ [14]

FROM
THE CATHOLIC CAMPAIGN FOR HUMAN DEVELOPMENT

From:
Poverty USA, http://www.povertyusa.org/poverty-resources/quiz/

1) The number of people living in poverty in the United States decreased from 2011 to 2012.
   a. True
   b. False

2) According to the US government, a family of four—two adults and two children—is living in poverty if it earns less than $28,000 annually.
   a. True
   b. False

3) Most people living in poverty are African American.
   a. True
   b. False

4) The federal minimum wage is $8.75 per hour.
   a. True
   b. False

5) The poverty rate among the elderly in the United States is higher than that of any other age group.
   a. True
   b. False

6) If every poor person in the United States in lived in the same state, it would be the most populous state in the nation—the State of Poverty.
   a. True
   b. False

7) In more than a dozen states the poverty rate is at least 1 out of 6 people.
   a. True
   b. False

8) In more than a dozen states the poverty rate is less than 10%.
   a. True
   b. False

ANSWERS

1) (b) False: In 2012 there was no statistical decrease in poverty for the second consecutive year.

2) (b) False: The federal "poverty threshold" in 2012 for a family of four with two children 17 or younger is $23,850. A family with a household income above that is not considered "poor." However, researchers estimate that, depending on locality, it takes an income of about 1.5 to 3.5 times the official poverty level to cover the cost of a family's minimum day-to-day needs.

3) (b) False: Based on the 2010 Census, over 19.5 million non-Hispanic white Americans lived below the poverty line in 2010. In the same year, there were 13.2 million Hispanics (of any race) in poverty, 10.7 million African Americans, and 1.7 million Asian Americans in poverty. As a percentage of the population, however, 27.4 percent of African Americans lived below the poverty line in 2010—the largest percentage of any group. 26.6 percent of Hispanics, 12.1 percent of Asian Americans, and 9.9 percent of non-Hispanic white Americans are living in poverty.

4) (b) False. The federal minimum wage became $7.25 per hour July 24, 2009. A single parent with one child

working at this minimum wage full-time every week of the year ($7.25 x 40 hours x 52 weeks) would earn $15,080 before any deductions or taxes. That is actually below the poverty line of $15,730 for a two-person family.

5) (b) False. Though the poverty rate for America's elderly (people over 65) rose from 8.9 percent in 2009 to 9.1 percent in 2012, the poverty rate for children under 18 is still higher, at 21.8 percent for 2012. That means more than 1 out of every 5 children in America lives in poverty.

6) (a) True. In 2012 the population in the State of Poverty was larger than the *combined* populations of Texas, New Mexico, Oklahoma, Kansas, Colorado, Arizona, Utah, Wyoming, Nevada, and Nebraska. 46.5 million Americans live in the State of Poverty, 8 million more people than in the State of California.

7) (a) True. According to 2012 figures, fourteen states have poverty rates above 16.6%: Arizona, Arkansas, Georgia, Kentucky, Louisiana, Mississippi, New Mexico, New York, North Carolina, Oklahoma, South Carolina, Tennessee, Texas, and West Virginia. The District of Columbia also has a poverty rate above 1 out of 6 residents.

8) (b) False. According to 2012 figures, only four states (Maryland, New Hampshire, New Jersey, and Wyoming) have a poverty line below 10%. Every other state in the nation has at least 1 out 10 persons living in poverty.

Data taken from websites sponsored by the Catholic Campaign for Human Development, *Poverty USA*, http://www.povertyusa .org/poverty-resources/quiz/ and from the U.S. Census Bureau, http://www.census.gov/.

Ten

CATHOLIC SOCIAL TEACHING

Selected Excerpts from Magisterial Documents

"To desire the common good and strive towards it is a requirement of justice and charity. . . . The more we strive to secure a common good corresponding to the real needs of our neighbors, the more effectively we love them. Every Christian is called to practice this charity, in a manner corresponding to his vocation and according to the degree of influence he wields in the [state]. This is the institutional path—we might also call it the political path—of charity, no less excellent and effective than the kind of charity which encounters the neighbor directly" (no. 7).

"Being out of work or dependent on public or private assistance for a prolonged period undermines the freedom and creativity of the person and his family and social relationships, causing great psychological and spiritual suffering. I would like to remind everyone, especially governments engaged in boosting the world's economic and social assets, that the primary capital to be safeguarded and valued is man, the human person in his or her integrity" (no. 25).

—*Charity in Truth* (*Caritas in Veritate*)
Pope Benedict XVI (2009)

"The Catholic way is to recognize the essential role and the complementary responsibilities of families, communities, the market, and government to work together to overcome poverty and advance human dignity" (p. 18).

—*A Place at the Table: A Catholic Recommitment to Overcome Poverty and to Respect the Dignity of All God's Children*
US Catholic Bishops (2002)

"The principle of subsidiarity reminds us that larger institutions in society should not overwhelm or interfere with smaller or local institutions, yet larger institutions have essential responsibilities when the more local institutions cannot adequately protect human dignity, meet human needs, and advance the common good" (no. 48).

"While the common good embraces all, those who are weak, vulnerable, and most in need deserve preferential concern. A basic moral test for our society is how we treat the most vulnerable in our midst" (no. 50).

—*Forming Consciences for Faithful Citizenship*
US Catholic Bishops (2007)

"The universal destination of goods requires that the poor, the marginalized and in all the cases those whose living conditions interfere with their proper growth should be the focus of particular concern" (no. 182).

"Solidarity without subsidiarity, in fact, can easily degenerate into a 'welfare state,' while subsidiarity without solidarity runs the risk of encouraging forms of self-centered localism. In order to respect both of these fundamental principles, the State's intervention in the economic environment must be neither invasive nor absent, but commensurate with society's real needs" (no. 351).

—*The Compendium of the Social Doctrine of the Church*
Pontifical Council for Justice and Peace (2005)

Eleven

THE OPTION FOR THE POOR IN CATHOLIC SOCIAL TEACHING

BY THOMAS MASSARO, SJ

From: *Living Justice: Catholic Social Teaching in Action*
(Rowman & Littlefield, 2012), 113–117.

In one sense, the notion of the *preferential option for the poor* is relatively new to Catholic social teaching, as this phrase appeared in no papal social encyclical until 1987 and in no official church documents at all until 1979. But in another sense, the preferential option for those who are poor and vulnerable has been present within the Christian tradition from the very start. The ministry of Jesus, in both words and deeds, was deeply wrapped up with this commitment to the well-being of the least fortunate. Making an option for the poor is not just a knee-jerk reaction to give the benefit of the doubt to those considered to be underdogs, but an abiding commitment, grounded in scripture and tradition, to support social justice by placing oneself on the side of the vulnerable and marginalized. . . .

Without using the precise phrase *preferential option for the poor*, the Church has long practiced this option in many ways, formal and informal, as it has placed concern for the most vulnerable members of society among its top priorities. . . .

From its very beginning, when nineteenth-century European social Catholicism started to notice and address the plight of hard-pressed working families, this tradition of social concern had consistently expressed the Church's mission to act as Jesus had acted in befriending the poor of his time. In fact, the 1991 encyclical *Ceniesimus Annus* contains a passage in which Pope John Paul II interprets *Rerum Novarum*'s call, a full century earlier, to improve the conditions of workers as a manifestation of the preferential option for the poor long before the phrase was coined. John Paul points to the similarity between the Church's role as advocate of the poor in 1891 and 1991 as evidence of the "church's constant concern for and dedication to categories of people who are especially beloved to the Lord Jesus" (no. 11). Indeed, throughout his long pontificate, John Paul II made frequent reference to this concept, phrased in various ways, as part of his trademark call to universal solidarity. Though by no means an uncritical proponent of liberation theology, the movement that originated the phrase *preferential option for the poor*, Pope John Paul II often raised up in his addresses and writings this social priority of working for the benefit of the least-advantaged members of society. . . . Many of his celebrated travels abroad, especially early in his reign as pope, featured visits to desperately impoverished neighborhoods where he publicized the need for greater solidarity between rich and poor around the world.

The imperative to make an option for the poor takes on distinctive features, of course, in the social context of the world's most affluent nations. Consider, for example, the significance of such an option within the United States, the richest society in the history of the world. Although tens of millions of Americans actually live below the federally defined poverty line, the extent and depth of poverty in the United States cannot compare to Latin America and similar parts of the developing world. Distressing social divisions are not nearly as profound in a society that is dominated by a middle-class ethos and where upward mobility, while never easy, is at least imaginably within the reach of citizens of quite modest means. Opportunities for advancement into the mainstream and even upper echelons of American society exist beyond the dreams of the vast majority of people living in other countries, who find most doors to a materially better life shut firmly against them.

What does it mean, then, in U.S. society, to make a preferential option for the poor? There are no easy answers, of course, as each individual must discern an appropriate personal response to this universal but imprecise call. Interestingly, in the course of their 1986 pastoral letter

Economic Justice for All, the U.S. Catholic bishops speak frequently of the option for the poor, mentioning the phrase explicitly nine times. Concern for the poor quite evidently pervades the entire letter, and the document urges lawmakers, citizens, consumers, and all others to measure all their decisions by the likely effects they will exert upon the least-advantaged members of society. To make a preferential option for the poor in a relatively affluent society may not entail an agenda of drastic social change to right a history of deep offenses against human solidarity, but it does probably mean much greater sensitivity to the impact one's actions exert upon the vulnerable and marginalized. In a largely middle-class society like America, making a sincere preferential option for the poor will lead people to revise their lifestyle choices and numerous personal decisions, as well as to advocate for public policies to advance social justice. This commitment might include greater support for progressive taxation measures, for social safety net programs to assist low-income families, and for better funding for educational services and schools that serve underprivileged neighborhoods.

The entire tradition of Catholic social teaching, . . . can be interpreted as a unified effort on the part of church leaders to advocate for a more humane society where the most vulnerable members are better protected from harm. With its limited financial resources, the Church itself can do only so much to advance the lives of the poor. However, popes and bishops, as the official voices of the Church, have exerted great efforts to speak publicly about political, economic, and social issues that have profound impact upon the prospects of our neediest neighbors. The rationale for all the Church's efforts in this regard may be summarized precisely as the desire to make a preferential option for the poor.

If these church efforts were to really bear fruit, then what would the results look like? If the message of justice and peace within Catholic social teaching were to take root in the hearts of many believers, these disciples would work energetically for a better world, a world characterized by not only acts of individual charity but also structures of justice and equity for all people. Racial discrimination and unfair barriers to progress would be eliminated. True human development would be fostered by wider access to property and by socially responsible policies of businesses and governments throughout the world. All social institutions, from schools to corporations to social clubs, would be measured by how they treat all members of society especially the poorest. Priorities would be altered so that more of the benefits of this abundantly blessed world would find their way to those who currently possess the least. In a prosperous age like the present one, no one should be excluded from enjoying an ample array of opportunities or be left to experience the disturbing fear of permanent powerlessness and deprivation.

Catholic social teaching includes a call for involvement in collaborative efforts to invite all people into the social mainstream; it is not an ethic for apathetic or complacent people. To adopt the principles of Catholic social thought is to concur that all people need to make sincere and vigorous efforts so that full participation is extended to all, without favoritism or discrimination. We all have something to contribute to the common good, and all may benefit from the gifts that we bring to the common table of human community and solidarity.

Twelve

CHRISTIAN FAMILIES IN CARE FOR THE POOR

BY JULIE HANLON RUBIO

From: *Family Ethics: Practices for Christians* (Washington, DC: Georgetown University Press, 2010), 164–165, 178–180, 183, 191–192, 204–209.

In this excerpt from her book on ethics and the family, a Catholic theologian, wife, and mother discusses two ways that Catholic families might demonstrate their concern for the poor.

TITHING

Most American Christian families think of themselves as somewhere in the broad middle on the scale of financial wellness. They know that they are not poor, for they do not struggle to pay for basics like food, clothing, or housing and enjoy certain luxuries. Yet they are also keenly aware that they are not as rich as some people they know, see, or read about, who drive fancy new cars or go on extravagant vacations. Like most Americans, they prefer to think of themselves as middle class. Yet the majority of American families have incomes that place them among the most privileged people in the world. . . .

Most of these families give some of their income away. . . . One can then estimate that approximately 3 percent of the income of Christian families is given to Churches, the less fortunate, schools, health care, the arts, and to those working for political change. Of this charitable giving, only about one-third goes to serve the needs of the poor.

Is it enough? Anyone who has pondered Jesus's sayings about wealth and has seen the suffering of the poor would probably answer no, but determining what would be enough remains a difficult task. . . . I argue that the practice of tithing is an appropriate response for most Christian families seeking to balance care of their own with biblical and traditional understandings of responsibility for the poor. . . .

A contemporary tithe would seek new ways to make concrete Christian obligations to aid the less fortunate and support one's local church. Thus a more nuanced and flexible notion of tithing is needed. . . . Even given necessary flexibility, the concept of a percentage remains helpful. . . . A percentage challenges families to make tithing a regular part of their budget, like a car payment or a 401 K plan, and it ensures that their giving will increase as their income grows. . . .

Christianity, which has included people of means from the earliest days of its existence, does not seem to require radical renunciation. It does, however, challenge everyone to question contemporary living standards, support the church, and come to the aid of the poor. It seems that 10 percent is a reasonable level of sacrifice, given the abundance most in our society enjoy and the manifold needs of the poor around the globe, though the wealthiest of families should be encouraged to give even more.

Why, then, do more families not tithe already? The difficulties of tithing in a consumerist society are considerable. One need not be unduly or uniformly gloomy about contemporary society to see the problem. A market economy is committed to growth and needs increasing consumption to thrive. Buying and having more seem unquestionable individual and social goods. In such a system, personal and social temperance is dismantled, so it becomes almost impossible to feel as though one has enough. So when families are asked in Catholic social teaching to give out of their excess, most feel they have little to give. . . .

Tithing is a practice with the power to check consumer culture. Certainly, it does not require embracing voluntary poverty and rejecting all unnecessary goods. However, for most families, giving 10 percent or more of their income will mean reversing "reference group upscaling" by living more simply than those around them. . . . Giving 10 percent or more does not require radical change, but it does require making small sacrifices. . . .

The choice of Christian families to practice resistance to poverty and overconsumption by tithing could have an enormous impact on the world. The problems of poverty are immensely complicated, and tithing alone cannot solve them. Nonetheless, it is a key part of a Christian ethic that recognizes abundance as a gift to be shared, links belief in Christ with attention to the least, and sees the potential of everyday practices to transform believers and the sinful social structures that inevitably distort that delight in the goods of creation that God enjoins upon all creatures.

SERVICE

Very few Catholic parents are in need of something more to do. . . . For the most part, middle-class American Catholics are hardworking, family centered, and devoted to the common good of their communities. They are engaged in plenty of service—to their children, their parents, and their parishes, as well as their children's schools, teams, and extracurricular groups. . . . Their gift of self to the persons they love is made concrete in hours at work to support their households and in the hundreds of small tasks, from laundry to coaching to carpooling, that fill their days. Though they have a great many more things than most people in the world, I would hesitate to say that they have lives consumed with having rather than being. The strongly negative characterizations of the literature on consumerism seem a poor fit.

And yet one can hear in the conversations of middle-class adults a certain dissatisfaction with this way of life, a yearning for a slower pace, deeper friendships, and more time to simply be with their spouses and their children. They are conscious of their relative privilege and of the waste of resources that middle-class life entails. They know their children do not really need more things and more activities. They wish they had more time to do something for the poor. They would like to spend more time in prayer or meditation. There is a certain emptiness that is evident amid the "fullness" of middle-class American suburban life, a suspicion that busyness does not allow us to live below the surface, a sense that this life is less than it ought to be. People are generally satisfied with their families and communities, but they know at some level that there is something missing.

This emptiness in busyness is, I argue, paradoxically connected to low expectations for marriage. Middle-class families expect suburban comfort, friendly local communities, and loving families, but the modern Catholic vision for marriage and family developed by John Paul II asks for much more than what most families would dare to imagine. . . . He gives families a mission to serve society, working to transform its unjust structures and soften its hard edges with works of charity, mercy, and hospitality. . . . This vision of John Paul II is lofty and inspiring. But given the heavy load most married people are carrying in trying to achieve a middle-class vision of happiness, it seems all but impossible.

However, I have suggested thus far that the work to which the pope calls families, the very work that seems as if it would burden families is in reality the work of communion and solidarity that will fulfill them. . . .

Service to the poor is important not just because it is commanded but because it is needed. When people close to our homes are hungry, suffering from violence, without shelter, or in need of jobs, of all the things we choose to do on a free evening or Saturday afternoon, service should have priority. . . .

Direct service works like nothing else to increase compassion, in part through encouraging a recognition of privilege. . . . Safe within the confines of middle- and upper-class neighborhoods, it is easy to feel as though everyone has as much or more than we do. Everyone we know is struggling to keep up with bills for tuition, extracurricular activities, clothes, home repair and remodeling, the modest yearly vacation, mortgage, utilities, and so forth. But walking into a shelter or soup kitchen throws our privilege into sharp relief: our shoes, haircuts, and jeans are of a different quality. Our cars look out of place. We are suddenly conscious of the value of our purses, wallets, or cellphones. Encountering those who are truly struggling enables us to think differently. . . .

Working directly with the poor reveals not only the privilege of the rich but also the poverty of the rich. . . . The poor teach us not only about poverty but also about how to live with gratitude and joy despite suffering. . . . When we see through regular contact with the poor that those with so much less than we have laugh, sing, dance, celebrate, and hope more than we are able to despite all our gifts, a new gratitude and joy can take root in us. This too can overflow in communion inside the family, in intimacy, in a willingness to sacrifice time and resources for others that is born of the same knowledge that our lives are very good. . . .

Direct service ought to be a central practice of Christian family life, a key way of resisting depersonalization in the home and outside it. . . . Being with those who have little and give much breaks through the numbness that is the sickness of our middle-class tribe, allowing joy, sadness, and passion to seep in. If families commit to this practice, they will find an antidote to "emptiness in busyness" in communion— in richer relationships at home, in community with fellow believers, in service to and friendship with those in need, and in a deeper sense of gratitude and connection to the God who made us all.

Thirteen

FEEDING THE POOR— AT A SACRIFICE

Teachings of Dorothy Day, Peter Maurin, and Jean Vanier

Peter Maurin

From: *Easy Essays* (Eugene, OR: Wipf & Stock, 2010).

FEEDING THE POOR—AT A SACRIFICE

In the first centuries
of Christianity
the hungry were fed
at a personal sacrifice,
the naked were clothed
at a personal sacrifice,
the homeless were sheltered
at personal sacrifice.
And because the poor
were fed, clothed and sheltered
at a personal sacrifice,

the pagans used to say

about the Christians

"See how they love each other."

In our own day

the poor are no longer

fed, clothed and sheltered

at a personal sacrifice,

at a personal sacrifice,

but at the expense

of the taxpayers.

And because the poor

are no longer

fed, clothed and sheltered

the pagans say about the Christians

"See how they pass the buck."

DOROTHY DAY

From: *Commonweal*, Nov. 4, 1949.

The spiritual works of mercy are: to admonish the sinner, to instruct the ignorant, to counsel the doubtful, to comfort the sorrowful, to bear wrongs patiently, to forgive all injuries, and to pray for the living and the dead.

The corporal works are to feed the hungry, to give drink to the thirsty, to clothe the naked, to ransom the captive, to harbor the harborless, to visit the sick, and to bury the dead.

When Peter Maurin talked about the necessity of practicing the works of mercy, he meant all of them, and he envisioned houses of hospitality in poor parishes in every city of the country, where these precepts of Our Lord could be put into effect. He pointed out that we have turned to State responsibility through home relief, social legislation and social security, and we no longer practice personal responsibility for our brother, but are repeating the words of the first murderer, "Am I my brother's keeper?" Not that our passing the buck is as crude as all that. . . .

Peter Maurin, the founder of *The Catholic Worker*, was very much an apostle to the world today, not only to the poor. He was a prophet with a social message and he wanted to reach the people with it. To get to the people, he pointed out it was necessary to embrace voluntary poverty, to strip yourself, which would give you the *means* to practice the works of mercy. To reach the man in the street you must go to the street. To reach the workers, you begin to study a philosophy of labor, and take up manual labor, useful labor, instead of white collar work. To be the least, to be the worker, to be poor, to take the lowest place and thus be the spark which would set afire the love of men towards each other and to God (and we can only show our love for God by our love for our fellows). These were Peter's ideas, and they are indispensable for the performing of the works of mercy. . . .

The works of mercy are a wonderful stimulus to our growth in faith as well as in love. Our faith is taxed to the utmost and so grows through this strain put upon it. It is pruned again and again, and springs up bearing much fruit. For anyone starting to live literally the words of the Fathers of the Church, "the bread you retain belongs to the hungry, the dress you lock up is the property of the naked," "what is superfluous for one's need is to be regarded as plunder if one retains it for one's self," there is always a trial ahead. "Our faith, more precious than gold, must be tried as though by fire." Here is a letter we received today. "I took a gentleman seemingly in need of spiritual and temporal guidance into my home on a Sunday afternoon. Let him have a nap on my bed, went through the want ads with him, made coffee and sandwiches for him, and when he left, I found my wallet had gone also."

I can only say that the Saints would only bow their heads and not try to understand or judge. They received no thanks—well then, God had to repay them. They forebore to judge, and it was as though they took off their cloak besides their coat to give away. This is expecting heroic charity of course. But these things happen for our discouragement, for our testing. We are sowing the seed of love, and we are not living in the harvest time so that we can expect a crop. We must love to the point of folly, and we are indeed fools, as our Lord Himself was who died for such a one as this. We lay down our lives too when we have performed so painfully thankless an act, because this correspondent of ours is poor in this world's goods. It is agony to go through such bitter experiences, because we all want to love, we desire with a great longing to love our fellows, and our hearts are often crushed at such rejections. But a Carmelite nun said to me last week, "It is the crushed heart which is the soft heart, the tender heart," and maybe it is one way to become meek and humble of heart like Jesus.

Such an experience is crueller than that of our young men in Baltimore who were arrested for running a disorderly house, i.e., our St. Anthony's house of hospitality, and who spent a few nights in jail. Such an experience is dramatic to say the least. Such an experience is crueller than that which happened to one of our men here in New York who was attacked (for his pacifism) by a maniac with a knife in our kitchen. Actually to shed one's blood is a less bitter experience.

Well, our friend has suffered from his experience and it is part of the bitterness of the poor, who cheat each other, who exploit each other, even as they are exploited. Who despise each other even as they are the despised.

And is it to be expected that virtue and destitution should go together? No, as John Cogley has written, they are the destitute in every way, destitute of this world's goods, destitute of honor, of gratitude, of love, and they need so much, that we cannot take the works of mercy apart, and say I will do this one, or that one work of mercy. We find they all go together.

Some years ago there was an article in *Commonweal* by Georges Bernanos. He ended his article as I shall end mine, paraphrasing his words, and it is a warning note for these apocalyptic times: "Every particle of Christ's divine charity is today more precious for your security—for your security, I say—than all the atom bombs in all the stock piles." It is by the works of mercy that we shall be judged.

Jean Vanier

From: *Essential Writings* (Maryknoll, NY: Orbis Books, 2008), 69, 105, 107.

When you are rich, when you have a name, when you have friends, or when you are a member of a respected group, you are never really oppressed. When in difficulty, simply make a telephone call and everything is fixed. I know this myself. I've never been really poor because I have enough friends and contacts. When you have no friends, when you are an immigrant and you speak the language badly, you are quickly oppressed, for you cannot defend yourself.

In the Gospels, there are the well-known "official" Beatitudes in Matthew and Luke, but there are other, more hidden Beatitudes throughout the Gospels. . . .

Blessed are those who eat with the poor (Luke 14); blessed are those who believe without seeing (John 20:29);

blessed are those who listen to the word of God and put it into practice (Luke 11:28). . . . And then there is the blessedness of washing each other's feet.

In the original Jerusalem Bible, the Greek word for "beatitude" was translated by "happy." That is not wrong, if we understand the deepest meaning of happiness. For it is truly a joy to wash the feet of the poor and weak, to live in communion with them. There is a deep but often hidden joy in being united to Jesus in his pain, tears, and rejection; to know that he is with us in it all. There is also an inner joy in discovering the meaning of all our suffering.

The rich man is rich precisely because he does not know how to give, because he does not know how to share. If he had known how to share he wouldn't be rich any longer. He who has shut himself into a world of defensiveness and pride cannot enter into the kingdom of sharing. The key to the kingdom, the only key, is openness: to open one's arms, one's eyes, one's heart, because the kingdom of God is just like that—the place of meeting, of communion, of peace, and of giving.

Fourteen

A CHURCH THAT IS POOR AND FOR THE POOR

by Pope Francis

From: *Evangelii Gaudium*, 58, 186–216.

The Pope loves everyone, rich and poor alike, but he is obliged in the name of Christ to remind all that the rich must help, respect and promote the poor. I exhort you to generous solidarity and to the return of economics and finance to an ethical approach which favors human beings. . . .

Our faith in Christ, who became poor, and was always close to the poor and the outcast, is the basis of our concern for the integral development of society's most neglected members.

Each individual Christian and every community is called to be an instrument of God for the liberation and promotion of the poor, and for enabling them to be fully a part of society. This demands that we be docile and attentive to the cry of the poor and to come to their aid. . . .

The Church has realized that the need to heed this plea is itself born of the liberating action of grace within each of us, and thus it is not a question of a mission reserved only to a few . . . it means working to eliminate the structural causes of poverty and to promote the integral development of the poor, as well as small daily acts of solidarity in meeting the real needs which we encounter. The word "solidarity" is a little worn and at times poorly understood, but it refers to something more than a few sporadic acts of generosity. It presumes the creation of a new mindset which thinks in terms of community and the priority of the life of all over the appropriation of goods by a few. . . .

We are not simply talking about ensuring nourishment or a "dignified sustenance" for all people, but also their "general temporal welfare and prosperity."[15] This means education, access to health care, and above all employment, for it is through free, creative, participatory and mutually supportive labor that human beings express and enhance the dignity of their lives. A just wage enables them to have adequate access to all the other goods which are destined for our common use. . . .

For the Church, the option for the poor is primarily a theological category rather than a cultural, sociological, political or philosophical one. God shows the poor "his first mercy."[16] This divine preference has consequences for the faith life of all Christians, since we are called to have "this mind . . . which was in Jesus Christ" (Phil 2:5). Inspired by this, the Church has made an option for the poor which is understood as a "special form of primacy in the exercise of Christian charity, to which the whole tradition of the Church bears witness."[17] This option— as Benedict XVI has taught—"is implicit in our Christian faith in a God who became poor for us, so as to enrich us with his poverty."[18] This is why I want a Church which is poor and for the poor. They have much to teach us. Not only do they share in the *sensus fidei*, but in their difficulties they know the suffering Christ. We need to let ourselves be evangelized by them. The new evangelization is an invitation to acknowledge the saving power at work in their lives and to put them at the centre of the Church's pilgrim way. We are called to find Christ in them, to lend our voice to their causes, but also to be their friends, to listen to them, to speak for them and to embrace the mysterious wisdom which God wishes to share with us through them.

Our commitment does not consist exclusively in activities or programs of promotion and assistance; what the Holy Spirit mobilizes is not an unruly activism, but above all an attentiveness which considers the other "in a certain sense as one with ourselves."[19] This loving attentiveness is the beginning of a true concern for their person which inspires me effectively to seek their good. This entails appreciating the poor in their goodness, in their experience of life, in their culture, and in their ways of living the faith. . . . The poor person, when loved, "is esteemed as of great value,"[20] and this is what makes the authentic option for the poor differ from any other ideology, from any attempt to exploit the poor for one's own personal or political interest. Only on the basis of this real and sincere closeness can we properly accompany the poor on their path of liberation. Only this will ensure that "in every Christian community the poor feel at home. Would not this approach be the greatest and most effective presentation of the good news of the kingdom?"[21] Without the preferential option for the poor, "the proclamation of the Gospel, which is itself the prime form of charity, risks being misunderstood or submerged by the ocean of words which daily engulfs us in today's society of mass communications."[22] . . .

The need to resolve the structural causes of poverty cannot be delayed, not only for the pragmatic reason of its urgency for the good order of society, but because society needs to be cured of a sickness which is weakening and frustrating it, and which can only lead to new crises. Welfare projects, which meet certain urgent needs, should be considered merely temporary responses. As long as the problems of the poor are not radically resolved by rejecting the absolute autonomy of markets and financial speculation and by attacking the structural causes of inequality,[23] no solution will be found for the world's problems or, for that matter, to any problems. Inequality is the root of social ills.

The dignity of each human person and the pursuit of the common good are concerns which ought to shape all economic policies. At times, however, they seem to be a mere addendum imported from without in order to fill out a political discourse lacking in perspectives or plans for true and integral development. How many words prove irksome to this system! It is irksome when the question of ethics is raised, when global solidarity is invoked, when the distribution of goods is mentioned, when reference is made to protecting labor and defending the dignity of the powerless, when allusion is made to a God who demands a commitment to justice. At other times these issues are exploited by a rhetoric which cheapens them. Casual indifference in the face of such questions empties our lives and our words of all meaning. Business is a vocation, and a noble vocation, provided that those engaged in it see themselves challenged by a greater meaning in life; this will enable them truly to serve the common good by striving to increase the goods of this world and to make them more accessible to all.

We can no longer trust in the unseen forces and the invisible hand of the market. Growth in justice requires more than economic growth, while presupposing such growth: it requires decisions, programs, mechanisms and processes specifically geared to a better distribution of income, the creation of sources of employment and an integral promotion of the poor which goes beyond a simple welfare mentality. . . .

Jesus, the evangelizer par excellence and the Gospel in person, identifies especially with the little ones (cf. Mt 25:40). This reminds us Christians that we are called to care for the vulnerable of the earth. But the current model, with its emphasis on success and self-reliance, does not appear to favor an investment in efforts to help the slow, the weak or the less talented to find opportunities in life.

It is essential to draw near to new forms of poverty and vulnerability, in which we are called to recognize the suffering Christ, even if this appears to bring us no tangible and immediate benefits. I think of the homeless, the addicted, refugees, indigenous peoples, the elderly who are increasingly isolated and abandoned, and many others. . . .

There are other weak and defenseless beings who are frequently at the mercy of economic interests or indiscriminate exploitation. I am speaking of creation as a whole. We human beings are not only the beneficiaries but also the stewards of other creatures. Thanks to our bodies, God has joined us so closely to the world around us that we can feel the desertification of the soil almost as a physical ailment, and the extinction of a species as a painful disfigurement. Let us not leave in our wake a swath of destruction and death which will affect our own lives and those of future generations.[24] . . .

Small yet strong in the love of God, like Saint Francis of Assisi, all of us, as Christians, are called to watch over and protect the fragile world in which we live, and all its peoples.

Notes

1 G. K. Chesterton, *St. Francis of Assisi* (Garden City: Doubleday Image Books, 1957), 96–97.

2 United States Census Bureau, "Poverty Thresholds," *United States Department of Commerce*, last modified Jan. 26, 2015, http://www.census.gov/hhes/www/poverty/data/threshld/.

3 United States Bureau of Labor Statistics, "A Profile of the Working Poor, 2012," *United States Department of Labor*, last modified March 2014, http://www.bls.gov/cps/cpswp2012.pdf.

4 Gordon M Fisher, "The Development and History of the Poverty Thresholds," *Social Security Bulletin 55*, no. 4 (1992): 3–14.

5 John Paul II, *Laborem Exercens* (1981), 4.

6 Ibid., 6.

7 Leo XIII, *Rerum Novarum* (1891), 45.

8 Lawrence Mishel, Josh Bivens, Elise Gould, and Heidi Shierholz, *The State of Working America*, 12th ed. (Ithaca, NY: Cornell University Press, 2012), 184, 189, 7, 236.

9 William Lazonick and Mary O'Sullivan, "Maximizing Shareholder Value: A New Ideology for Corporate Governance," *Economy and Society* 29, no. 1 (2000): 13–35.

10 Quoted in C. Melissa Snarr, *All You That Labor: Religion and Ethics in the Living Wage Movement* (New York: New York University Press, 2011), 41; see also Stephanie Luce, *Fighting for a Living Wage* (Ithaca, NY: ILR Press, 2004), 48.

11 See Leo XIII, *Rerum Novarum*, 46; John A. Ryan, *A Living Wage: Its Ethical and Economic Aspects* (New York: Macmillan, 1906), especially 117–119.

12 Ben Craig and John Pencavel, "The Behavior of Worker Cooperatives: The Plywood Companies of the Pacific Northwest," *The American Economic Review* 82, no. 5 (1992): 1083–1105.

13 Ben Craig and John Pencavel, "The Objectives of Worker Cooperatives," *Journal of Comparative Economics* 17, no. 2 (1993): 288–308.

14 Based on most recent reliable U.S. Census Bureau figures for the year 2012.

15 Paul VI, *Populorum Progressio*, 65.

16 John Paul II, "Homily at Mass for the Evangelization of Peoples in Santo Domingo" (11 Oct. 1984), 5: AAS 77 (1985), 358.

17 John Paul II, *Solllicitudo Rei Socialis*, 42.

18 "Address at the Inaugural Session of the Fifth General Conference of the Latin American and Caribbean Bishops" (13 May 2007), 3: AAS 99 (2007), 450.

19 Thomas Aquinas, *Summa Theologica* II–II.27.2.

20 Ibid., I–II.26.3.

21 John Paul II, *Novo Millennio Ineunte*, 50.

22 Ibid.

23 This implies a commitment to "eliminate the structural causes of global economic dysfunction," Benedict XVI, *Address to the Diplomatic Corps* (8 Jan. 2007): AAS 99 (2007), 73.

24 Cf. *Propositio* 56.

About Paraclete Press

WHO WE ARE

As the publishing arm of the Community of Jesus, Paraclete Press presents a full expression of Christian belief and practice—from Catholic to Evangelical, from Protestant to Orthodox, reflecting the ecumenical charism of the Community and its dedication to sacred music, the fine arts, and the written word. We publish books, recordings, sheet music, and DVDs that nourish the vibrant life of the church and its people.

WHAT WE ARE DOING
Books

PARACLETE PRESS BOOKS show the richness and depth of what it means to be Christian. While Benedictine spirituality is at the heart of who we are and all that we do, our books reflect the Christian experience across many cultures, time periods, and houses of worship.

We have many series, including *Paraclete Essentials*; *Paraclete Fiction*; *Paraclete Giants*; and the new *The Essentials of...*, devoted to Christian classics. Others include *Voices from the Monastery* (men and women monastics writing about living a spiritual life today), *Active Prayer*, the award-winning *Paraclete Poetry*, and new for young readers: *The Pope's Cat*. We also specialize in gift books for children on the occasions of Baptism and First Communion, as well as other important times in a child's life, and books that bring creativity and liveliness to any adult spiritual life.

The MOUNT TABOR BOOKS series focuses on the arts and literature as well as liturgical worship and spirituality; it was created in conjunction with the Mount Tabor Ecumenical Centre for Art and Spirituality in Barga, Italy.

Music

The PARACLETE RECORDINGS label represents the internationally acclaimed choir *Gloriæ Dei Cantores*, the *Gloriæ Dei Cantores Schola*, and the other instrumental artists of the *Arts Empowering Life Foundation*.

Paraclete Press is the exclusive North American distributor for the Gregorian chant recordings from St. Peter's Abbey in Solesmes, France. Paraclete also carries all of the Solesmes chant publications for Mass and the Divine Office, as well as their academic research publications.

In addition, PARACLETE PRESS SHEET MUSIC publishes the work of today's finest composers of sacred choral music, annually reviewing over 1,000 works and releasing between 40 and 60 works for both choir and organ.

Video

Our DVDs offer spiritual help, healing, and biblical guidance for a broad range of life issues including grief and loss, marriage, forgiveness, facing death, understanding suicide, bullying, addictions, Alzheimer's, and Christian formation.

Learn more about us at our website:
www.paracletepress.com

or phone us toll-free at 1.800.451.5006

SCAN
TO
READ
MORE